20 19 18 17 16   5 4 3 2 1

Text and photographs © 2016 by Steve Gross and Susan Daley

Published by
Gibbs Smith
P.O. Box 667
Layton, Utah 84041

1.800.835.4993 orders
www.gibbs-smith.com

Designed by Katie Jennings
Pages produced by Melissa Dymock

Gibbs Smith books are printed on paper produced from sustainable PEFC-certified forest/controlled wood source. Learn more at www.pefc.org.
Printed and bound in Hong Kong

Library of Congress Cataloging-in-Publication Data

Gross, Steve, author.
  The creative cottage / Steve Gross and Susan Daley. — First Edition.
     pages cm
  ISBN 978-1-4236-3848-3
1. Interior decoration—United States—Themes, motives.
2. Cottages—United States—Themes, motives. I. Daley, Susan, 1953– author. II. Title.
  NK2002.G7665 2016
  747'.880973—dc23
                                        2015028096

Contents

Introduction

"I had rather be shut up in a very modest cottage with my books, my family and a few old friends, dining on simple bacon, and letting the world roll on as it liked, than to occupy the most splendid post, which any human power can give." —Thomas Jefferson

BEACH HOUSE, FARMHOUSE, SALTBOX OR CABIN—what makes a cottage? This is the question we were often asked in the year we spent photographing a variety of cottages for this book.

We found that what defines a cottage is much more than just an architectural type or style of dwelling. A good cottage is a home with a sensibility of mind and place that suggests comfort and simplicity, where modesty of scale and avoidance of pretense afford the freedom to live according to personal desires and tastes.

As Jefferson believed, a cottage is a place where richness is to be found in the luxuries of time and privacy, a place in which to garden, read, cook and enjoy life's pleasures. Out of a fairly modest place, extraordinary things can come.

The cottages we discovered for this book are the homes of artists, preservationists and visionaries, people with creative abilities and imagination. They are not furnished according to any one period or style, but have evolved over years as a collage of things from different eras, containing old and new elements that come together to create a pleasing whole.

Although the homeowners show a proclivity for timeworn things that come from the past, they also exhibit a modern translation of decor and current tastes. From minimally furnished to ornately decorated

ones, the houses have the strong tactile qualities of rough wood and beams, patched floors, creaky stairs and much patina.

Inside, the furnishings draw on memories, history and reminiscences and act as repositories of favorite things. There is a plenitude of art objects, books, heirlooms, vintage collections, painted murals, handmade wallpapers and homemade furniture, as well as the wood-burning stoves and fireplaces, the geraniums on the windowsills, and the cozy nooks and cupboards usually associated with cottage life.

The houses shown are, in general, all fairly old ones, with the inhabitants liking things to look their age and having the understanding that an old house must be allowed to look like one, although anachronisms and modern conveniences are allowed. Some of the buildings did not actually even start out as cottages; there is a beach house that used to be a ship captain's warehouse, and a country house that used to be a blacksmith's forge. But they were cleverly transformed into cottages by people who knew how to gently alter them and furnish them in a cottage-like spirit.

The homeowners have added on to their buildings with new rooms, walls, floors, ceilings and windows, as well as having subtracted the same, sometimes stripping away to leave only the bare essentials. They have discerned how to ingeniously make the most of small

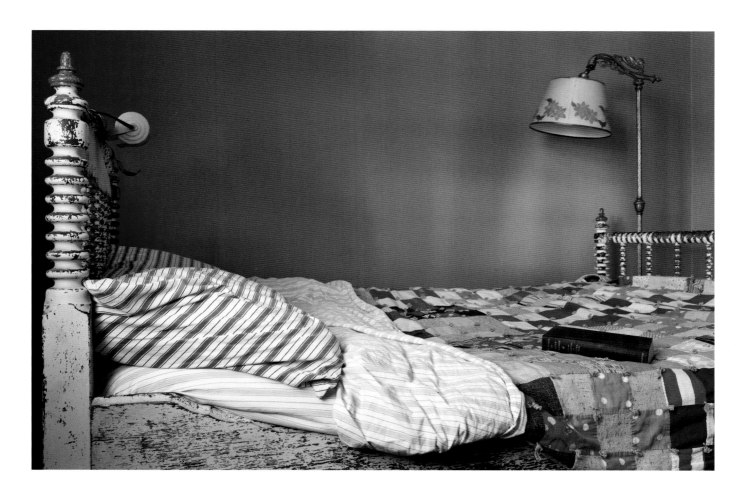

spaces, according to their desires and needs. It is a constantly changing process of renovation and revival.

As cottages are generally rural, the houses also share a deep connection with the outdoors, and are on intimate terms with their natural environments, fitting well into their surrounding landscapes. Some have half-wild gardens or box-lined patios, some have screened porches for sitting and dining, and some have French doors that open out to blend indoors with outdoors easily. One of the chief luxuries of liv-

ing in these places is being in close contact with nature and enjoying the views and the changing of seasons.

There will always be a longing for some people to escape to a small cottage situated in a forgotten village, perched on top of a forested mountain, hidden down a dirt road or clinging to the rocks beside the sea, like the ones shown in this book. We hope that these examples will inspire you to see the intrinsic beauty and possibilities of simple dwellings and to create your own outstanding version of the cottage.

Cape Cod Revival

LANDSCAPE PAINTER JOHN DOWD inhabits a 1750 cottage in Provincetown, an old seacoast town on the tip of Cape Cod. The town, which has been a whaling port, a Portuguese fishing village, a beach resort and a major art colony, has long attracted an array of artists, writers, eccentrics and visionaries, who brought with them an imaginative lifestyle.

Drawn there by the ocean light and the picturesque surroundings, artists found they could stay in inexpensive boarding houses and rent studios very cheaply. In the same way, Dowd came to Provincetown the summer after he graduated from Notre Dame's School of Architecture, and worked at a guesthouse in exchange for free rent.

He began painting buildings in landscapes instead of designing houses and eventually found himself buying an old cottage that had been on the market for years. The house was "unwanted, unloved, and covered in ugly aluminum siding," which, to his relief, "all peeled off in one afternoon, like foil on a baked potato."

Though the house "was not attractive in any way, it was big enough to have an art studio," and John felt there was character lurking behind some unsightly renovations. His idea was not to undertake a total makeover. Instead, he set out to put the house "back the way it used to be, on a budget of just about zero," using building materials he mainly found or salvaged.

Having in his mind a memory of his grandparents' antique-filled Victorian to emulate, and with an artist's eye for detail, he haunted salvage yards and junk shops. Things began to come to him serendipitously, finding their way to the house and settling in, looking like they'd been there for a hundred years or more.

Fortuitously, John happened to find an elegant mantel and china cabinet from a similar Cape Cod cottage that fit perfectly into his own living room, which was missing those elements. For the kitchen, he came upon an old woodstove and a Victorian table like the ones he remembered from his childhood.

Reclaiming used things that had been rejected by others, John realized that what he liked best about them were "the imperfections, which is what makes them more interesting." His house today serves not only as a repository of his personal memories but also as a small archive of Provincetown art history. Hanging on his walls *salon* style are paintings by a legion of Cape Cod artists who migrated to Provincetown since the late 1800s, when its art colony began.

Weaving his sense of beauty and history together, John has composed a home with rooms that are both nostalgic and poetic. "The house is my greatest art piece, my most creative work," he says. "In it, I've used my architectural skills, my love of art, my childhood memories and put it all together in a construction that constantly changes over the years."

In the upstairs parlor, pine floorboards have been left bare. John found the paint "ghosts" of antique iron hardware that had originally been on the doors and traced their shapes in order to help locate ones that exactly matched.

John Dowd added green shutters and screen doors, as well as salvaged panes of old wavy glass, to his Cape Cod cottage in Provincetown. The picturesquely asymmetrical house was once a favorite of vintage postcard publishers.

OPPOSITE ABOVE: *An upstairs parlor used to be the main bedroom of the house. With so many of its original features intact, John says, it was "the least molested or altered room in the house."*

OPPOSITE BELOW: *A "sweetly stylized" seagull painting done by John Floyd Clymer in the 1920s hangs above a shallow fireplace, now boarded up. The mantel displays an 1860s harpoon, a relic of the whale hunts that brought prosperity to old Provincetown.*

OPPOSITE: *A small dormer room contains a captain's bed, a firehouse Windsor chair and not much else. John added the plaid curtains surrounding the bed, saying it reminds him of train travel.*

ABOVE: *The bunk room's three brass beds were acquired one at a time. "Although they've gone out of fashion, the beds are good and strong," says John, "and just seem to fit the room."*

RIGHT: *John usually has guests staying in the house, sleeping in beds with the brass left unpolished in favor of an acquired patina. Shelves in the upstairs hall house a collection of art books that overflow onto Hitchcock chairs.*

From the window of the upstairs hall, a bust of Shakespeare looks down upon the street. A painting of the old Route 66 Lincoln Highway to the West Coast hangs next to a tourist sign from one of the local guesthouses.

OPPOSITE: To partition an alcove of the living room, John hung striped, twin-sized bedspreads as curtains, creating a "book nook." He found the neo-Gothic transom at a salvage yard.

OPPOSITE: *A blue-and-white homespun coverlet, a hooked rug and handmade lace curtains create an "old Massachusetts" ambience in the downstairs bedroom.*

ABOVE: *Wanting his house to feel like a multigenerational New England family home, John furnished it with pieces from different eras, such as a Windsor chair, a butler's table and an Empire sofa.*

LEFT: *In a Truro thrift shop, John found a painting depicting a view of Provincetown's sinuous paths and beach dunes circa 1915. "The painting and frame found each other ten years later," after John purchased them at separate times and they were reunited purely by chance.*

OPPOSITE ABOVE: *A comfortable chaise is covered with a plaid for "winter dress" in a corner of the living room. John likes to "wallpaper the wall with paintings" and has collected art from the first decades of Provincetown's art colony.*

OPPOSITE BELOW: *The downstairs bedroom was one of two "side parlors" in the house. Above the desk, a Currier and Ives print shows the 1883 steamboat Pilgrim, which went from New York to Boston.*

LEFT: *At the end of a day at the Brimfield flea market, no one wanted to buy the large white cabinet and John was able to purchase it for $40, strap it on top of his Volvo and bring it home.*

RIGHT: *The china cabinet was salvaged from a similar old Cape Cod and installed by John in the living room of his house. It holds a collection of Sheffield plates, tarnished silver, and Sandwich glass.*

John wanted the kitchen, which was last modernized in the 1950s, to look "much older and not too fancy, not too rustic." The walnut table is "just one of those omnipresent nineteenth-century, middle-class tables you see everywhere."

RIGHT: A general store lantern with tarnished tin shade has been converted to electricity from kerosene. John placed an old, heavy enameled sink into a butcher board counter; both were salvage items.

OPPOSITE: John found a 1910 stove in working condition at a yard sale in Dorchester. The same day he also found some old wood paneling that he reassembled on the wall behind the stove. The gingerbread shelf clock came from his grandparents' house.

DeJoux Cottage

"ONE OF THE AMAZING THINGS about owning a 270-year-old house is that at every turn there is a mysterious fact that needs investigating," says William Chardock.

Many things have come to light since 2009 when William, an advertising specialist, and architect Daniel Flebut first bought the stone cottage in the Hudson Valley hamlet of Springtown, New York. Nearly every week there has been a surprise—some delightful, some not.

When they first acquired the place, it was buried so deeply in overgrowth that they could barely get to it. They knew it needed lots of love and attention, but they also knew that falling for a neglected old house can be nothing but trouble. They decided they would try to keep the cottage's old-world character while adding some crucial modern improvements of their own.

After many trips to the local library and discussions with town historians, William and Daniel learned their house had been built in 1755 by Christoffel DeJoux and was first inhabited by DeJoux and his wife Deborah, along with their children and five slaves. The DeJoux family was part of a group of Huguenots fleeing religious persecution who settled in Springtown, on the banks of the Wallkill River. Though the DeJoux were French, the cottage was built in the Hudson Valley's Dutch colonial vernacular style, with staunch rafters, double doors, an upstairs granary loft, deep casement windows and two jambless fireplaces.

William and Daniel also discovered that another former owner had been a partner of the famed Colony restaurant in New York City, and that he had left behind for them to find "an aged bottle of Perry, an alcoholic sparkling pear cider popular in the 1940s, along with a silver smelling salts bottle."

Built into a kitchen wall, they came upon an old beehive oven, full of cobwebs and with its bricks falling in, and began to restore it. Next to it they placed a big Aga stove that "in all its glory, weighs half a ton and had to be assembled piece by piece," says William.

With machetes, the couple began to tame the wilderness and cut a path around the perimeter of the property, uncovering gooseberry and currant bushes in the process and finding asparagus beds and mushrooms. They discovered an old orchard with over thirty types of fruit trees, including pears and paw paws. They learned how to cope with spring floods and how to wage wars against beavers, poison ivy and mosquitoes.

Along the way, they established their aesthetic of fusing past and present, furnishing the house in a minimal, modern way that was still in keeping with its original Huguenot simplicity, and meanwhile relishing all the quirks of an ancient house.

"The house has not changed in some ways, and in others it is all entirely new," says William. "The original features we discovered and restored are front and center. The house is cleaner, simpler and more like it would have been in the eighteenth century, but it is also contemporary. But it's still the same house that we both fell in love with."

The loft door of a second floor bedroom was kept and updated with glass, an example of the owners' philosophy of "modernizing with respect to the vernacular."

ABOVE: *Built in 1755 by French Huguenots in the Dutch colonial vernacular style, the cottage contained a grain loft on its second story.*

BELOW: *The back porch had been closed in with windows and paneling before William and Daniel opened it up with screening. This airy space is where the couple "practically live all summer, relaxing, working, dining and entertaining."*

Behind the DeJoux cottage, a large spring-fed pond was dug out from a boggy area in the 1980s. The site of the house was originally determined by Munsee Native Americans to be safe from spring floods.

LEFT: *A Jotul wood stove originally stood in the kitchen. Moving it to the dining room, William and Daniel used unglazed porcelain tile salvaged from a barn in France to create the floor around it.*

RIGHT: *An antique Polish jug from London sits on the casement windowsill; in some places, the walls of the house are two feet thick. The stools are new and were built by an artisanal furniture company in the Catskills.*

OPPOSITE ABOVE: *Scraping and cleaning the ceiling beams "of their many layers of soot, tar and paint was the hardest job of the restoration," William says. The paneled wall behind the high-backed settee is hand-finished and intentionally left a little rough.*

OPPOSITE BELOW: *A dining area was created next to a casement window using a Knoll table fitted with a new marble top in combination with vintage 1960s Arne Jacobsen bentwood chairs from a New York City flea market.*

The kitchen, which is "two rooms knocked together," has a massive trestle table made by William out of sawhorses and floorboards from an old factory in Pennsylvania.

OPPOSITE ABOVE: A kitchen addition made to the house in 1765 included a dome-shaped beehive oven, which had long been dismantled. The couple had cabinets made of limed oak.

OPPOSITE BELOW: At one time there was a characteristic Dutch jambless fireplace where the new Aga stove now sits. William, who grew up with an Aga in England, remembers farm cottages where the radiant heat of an Aga would warm and bring life to the entire house.

The purpose of the glass windows in the bedroom
doors remains a mystery. William and Daniel decided
to keep them, wanting to retain as many of the
characteristic quirks of the original house as possible.

In an upstairs bedroom, oak planks cut from a next-door neighbor's tree are outlined from behind with black tar paper. A 1950s Paul McCobb console was a find at a local estate sale, with the legs having been slightly altered.

OPPOSITE: *Until screen doors were invented, the popularity of the Dutch door in America was unrivaled. It allowed fresh air into the house while keeping stray farm animals out.*

The fireplace in the living room was rebuilt using the original handmade bricks, with Daniel designing the mantel to look like it had always been there. The room contains an anesthesiologist's cart, now serving as a drinks table.

Blue Shutters

"IT'S JUST LIKE LIVING ON A BOAT, but, thank God, without the boat," says Stephen Score, owner of the Provincetown, Massachusetts, cottage known as Blue Shutters. "It's more on water than on land, and all awash in light, and there is always a view of the sea everywhere you look." On the other hand, his wife, Eleanor, who grew up sailing, has been eyeing the empty davits on the wharf and thinking she may have plans for a boat, after all.

The weather-beaten gray cottage was built c. 1840 as the wharf head building for N. C. Brooks, a merchant of lumber, groceries, wood and straw and sits upon its own small wharf reaching out into Cape Cod Bay. It has always been oriented towards the bay since life in this town has long revolved around the commercial waterfront. On the wharves, fishermen and merchants combed through all manner of things having to do with the sea; codfish was filleted, lobsters and oysters were sold, mackerel was packed and whale schooners were built and repaired.

And because the house was so close to the water, yet set back from the street and quite secluded, people would stop to look through the privets at the mysterious house with the faded blue shutters that had sat vacant for a dozen or so years but had never been offered for sale.

The cottage had been occupied since 1953 by artists Jacques and Florence Salvan. Beginning in the 1930s a themed nautical décor had sprung up in Provincetown, promulgated nationally by Cape Cod style authority and folk artist Peter Hunt, who employed young artists to decoratively paint the furnishings he sold in his shop. Based on folk art and the trappings of fishing and paraphernalia of a seafaring culture, such things as lobster traps, chowder pots, fishing nets, buoys and ship's wheels began to be encouraged and admired as objects of adornment.

In like manner, the Salvans developed a maritime theme for their cottage. Jacques painted murals depicting coastal scenery, shells, harbors, a mermaid rising from the ocean and an angel poised as a ship's masthead. A painting by Florence of a lobster seafood dinner decorated their icebox; a bedroom contained a small shrine dedicated to Our Lady, Star of the Sea. Porthole windows were built into their galley kitchen and a ship's ladder was used to access the top floor

Today, after purchasing the house, Stephen and Eleanor say they have no interest in changing the nautical look of the cottage with its knotty pine walls and ocean blue floors. They decided they would keep the furnishings the Salvans had left behind, gradually adding in pieces of their own extensive folk art collection; objects that Stephen says "are joyful and happy and delightful to live with." Along with the things inherited from the Salvans, a home was created with a distinct sense of humor and whimsy, "a place that feels like an antidote to the heaviness and seriousness of the world." A place where the doors are left open and ocean breezes blow through, and where the sea is always within view.

The third-floor room, with knotty pine walls and a balcony deck facing the bay, was Jacques Salvan's art studio; Eleanor Score paints here today.

LEFT: *The street side of Stephen and Eleanor Score's cottage has French doors and white curtains blowing in the ocean breeze. When the doors are open at both ends you can see right through the house to the water and the boats sailing by.*

ABOVE: *The faded blue shutters are what first attracted the Scores to the house. Ball-fringed curtains were sewn by Florence Salvan.*

OPPOSITE: *A deck overlooks Cape Cod Bay on every floor of the Provincetown cottage. The bottom deck extends out over the beach on pilings so that sitting there is "like being on a ship at sea."*

OPPOSITE. *In the living room, a mural of ships in a French harbor was painted by Jacques Salvan; his wife, Florence, acted as the model for the angel and the mermaid. Stephen says "the intensely red Windsor arm chair came out of deepest, darkest New Hampshire."*

ABOVE: *The main room of the house has French doors opening onto a spacious deck overlooking the water.*

LEFT. *Contemporary artist Eleanor Score made the collage showing the main pier of Provincetown. The barrel was painted by folk artist Peter Hunt; a huge clothespin on the door of a closet is another piece of folk art.*

The dining room table and Windsor chairs are additions made by the Scores. The curtains, patterned with sailboats, were there when they moved in.

RIGHT: *In the attic, the Scores found an enamel icebox door illustrated by Florence Salvan with a fanciful Parisian seafood meal of lobster, oysters and wine.*

OPPOSITE ABOVE: *The galley kitchen is small but has everything one needs. "If you must wash dishes, you'll get to look out at sailboats and the moon rising over the water," says Stephen.*

OPPOSITE BELOW: *Porthole windows were built into the galley kitchen to reference seafaring. The cubbyhole shelving, which is a work of art in itself, holds glasses decorated with stripes, polka dots, and people driving 1920s cars.*

Two sandpipers touch beaks on an American hooked rug above the bed in an upstairs bedroom. An 1820s quilt from Maine, patterned with birds and leafy fronds, and a chenille spread cover the bed.

In the spaces under the eaves, fishnets, oars, buoys, lanterns and discarded pieces of furniture were found—a trove of decorative objects. A folding ship's ladder with a rope to hold onto is the way down.

LEFT: *In the corner of a small guest bedroom, the Salvans devoted a shrine to Our Lady, Star of the Sea, who is believed to intercede as protector for all those who seek their livelihoods at sea.*

OPPOSITE: *For this tiny bedroom, the Scores had boat-size beds made to fit at a ship-outfitting store in Salem. The small headboards were constructed by Stephen out of two table leaves found in the attic.*

RIGHT: *Of humble things such as this bedside lamp, Stephen says, "Beauty and integrity can be found in simple, common things that do not cost a fortune." A conch shell held aloft by a rope and a bit of spiral-painted pottery date from the Salvan days.*

Artists' Haven

PIETRO NIVOLA GREW UP in a 1754 cedar-shingled house filled with vibrant art in Springs, New York, a small town on the East End of Long Island. Today, after inheriting his childhood home, he is living there again along with his wife, Katherine Stahl.

Pietro's parents, Costantino "Tino" and Ruth Nivola, were among the influx of artists from New York City who managed to acquire inexpensive, somewhat dilapidated cottages available in this beach town in the years soon after World War II. The Nivolas were part of an avant-garde art milieu that included the de Koonings, Mark Rothko, Saul Steinberg, Lee Krasner, Jackson Pollock and others, all of whom came to escape the city and to paint, draw and sculpt close to the sea and sand dunes. In Springs, the artists found a more casual, easy-going lifestyle of swimming, clambakes and informal get-togethers, much of it based around the Nivolas' home where they congregated.

Pietro was given his first bicycle by Jackson Pollock and remembers going for rides with him in his Model A. As a weekend guest, the architect Le Corbusier swiftly painted two commanding murals on the living room walls. Bernard Rudofsky helped Pietro's father design Mediterranean-style gardens filled with "outdoor rooms," pergolas, sculptures, and a solarium, along with a traditional Sardinian baking oven.

The son of a master stonemason, Tino was born and grew up in Orani, a rural village in Sardinia where he learned to work as an artisan with humble materials such as stone, clay, tin and sand. Along with his wife, Ruth, whom he met while they were both art students in Milan, Tino completely transformed the Springs property after buying it from a lighthouse keeper. He tore down some walls and painted the rest white, with floors done in chrome yellow, infusing the house with light, air and color. He turned the old horse barn into his studio, where he made sculptures drawing upon the archaic forms of his ancestors.

Beginning in 2011, Pietro and Katherine continued the revitalizing process, managing to retain the spirit of the place while making some crucial improvements of their own. They moved the house, which had been built in a swale and subject to frequent flooding, back one hundred feet to higher ground, thus keeping its famed murals from danger. They removed the dilapidated kitchen and built a big, bright new addition in its place They remodeled the barn that had been Tino's studio into a capacious guesthouse, leaving the rough wood walls and old beams intact.

Using their own artistic sensibilities, Pietro and Katherine created a striking modernist décor which still has its roots in an old-world ambience. The emblematic bright yellow floors, red-painted rocking chair and Sardinian baskets from his parents' time are still there. And so is the fusion of art and architecture. Their house continues to be imbued with what Tino, called "the vitalizing touch of the artist, the touch that humanizes a building, which must always be present to create a life-enhancing environment," for now and future generations.

The biomorphic mural was painted directly onto the plaster wall by architect Le Corbusier, adding drama to the house.

ABOVE: *A brick-floored patio is covered by an old trumpet vine, which over the years has grown into one of Tino Nivola's sand-cast cement sculptures.*

BELOW: *The garden design merges landscape and architecture, with different open air "rooms" created of masonry walls. Along with a Sardinian oven, Tino built a freestanding fireplace with chimney for outdoor cooking.*

Bernard Rudofsky, an Austrian architect known for his work on vernacular architecture, collaborated with his friend Tino on the design of the garden. A horizontally slatted fence defines space, while a wisteria-covered pergola acts as an extension of the house.

OPPOSITE ABOVE: *Above a bookcase is a maquette of the monumental, 75-foot-long sand-cast frieze that Tino made for the Olivetti showroom in Manhattan in the 1950s. The relief was modeled in sand and then cast in plaster according to a technique developed while watching his children make sand castles on the beach.*

OPPOSITE BELOW: *Tino liked to use industrial paint colors, such as this "bulldozer yellow." He also employed Mediterranean blue for a calming effect.*

ABOVE: *In the living room, hand-hewn beams have been retained and the room is punctuated with bright colors and artworks, including a painting by Josef Albers. In the corner sits a statue by Tino, one of a series of stylized female figures.*

Pietro Nivola and a local architect designed a large, open kitchen addition to replace the old one. Copper pans and a turquoise teapot once belonged to Ruth Nivola.

RIGHT: *Le Corbusier often spent time with the Nivola family. One summer weekend, on an impulse, he painted two murals on adjacent walls, using "leftover house paint and every other kind of paint he could find in Tino's studio," says Pietro.*

OPPOSITE: *A huge black coal stove that once dominated the kitchen is gone, but a red rocking chair and Sardinian baskets provide links to the past. Tino built the tall, stacked cupboard with screening for storing fruits and vegetables.*

OPPOSITE: *Ruth Nivola used a small converted outbuilding as her art studio. Inspired by a trip abroad, her daughter Claire, who is an artist and book illustrator, painted murals on the walls depicting scenes in a Grecian town.*

ABOVE: *On the third floor, an unused attic was converted into a studio for Katherine and includes a spool bed that was once her mother's. Above it is a painting by Adrian Nivola of his grandmother Ruth, an artist who created exotic filigree jewelry.*

LEFT: *The upstairs bathroom still has the original tub, but another window has been added to enable soaking while enjoying a view of the garden.*

OPPOSITE ABOVE. *In a corner of the barn, one of Tino's small, sculpted figures was cut with metalsmith's scissors out of tin. A painting of a cottage with a blue door by the sea in Maine is the one piece of art in the house that came from Katherine's family.*

OPPOSITE BELOW. *In many artists' homes in Springs, barns were often utilized as studios and summer sleeping quarters. Originally the barn had a dirt floor that Tino covered in brick; today it has pine flooring painted white.*

Katherine and Pietro have renovated the old barn into a guest house, adding tall bookshelves, a large square coffee table made by Tino, a Norman Bluhm painting and a rug woven in Sardinia after one of Tino's images.

DIY Cottage

BUTCH ANTHONY, A SELF-DESCRIBED ARTIST, picker and builder of things, lives in a house he made by hand on his family's eighty-acre farm in Seale, Alabama. In his grandfather's time, they grew cotton and raised chickens on the land. Today the farm is a compound that includes Butch's house, his parents' 1950s ranch house, the Possum Trot Auction place, and the Museum of Wonder, a kind of roadside attraction filled with folk art and curiosities.

Built into the side of a gently sloping hill, the house Butch made is sturdily constructed of heart pine timbers he salvaged from an old cotton mill in Georgia. Butch had no formal architectural plan in mind when he began work on the dwelling in 1988; as he says he "just started nailing." Wearing out three chain saws in the process of splitting 12 x 12-foot salvaged timbers in half, Butch devised a homemade rigging system for raising the beams by stringing cables and pulleys from the branches of nearby pine trees.

Using reclaimed and scavenged materials, such as windows salvaged from old churches and columns rescued from torn-down Victorian porches, the entire structure is "intertwangled," the term Butch uses to describe mixing things together with a "twang" in order to form something unique.

Within the house, the furnishings have been intertwangled as well. Just about everything has been made by Butch himself, with the rest having been traded for or found on his rambles to junk shops, dumps and auctions. "I just can't quit picking stuff up," he says, "Every time I go to the dump, I come back with more than I went with."

The detritus of everyday life is ingeniously reassembled into a one-of-a-kind, richly patinated environment. Butch picks up vintage stools "for a couple of bucks each whenever they come through at auction" and finds old carpenters' toolboxes that can serve as end tables. He spots an element such as an elegant mantel painted bright pink in an abandoned shack and brings it home, strips the paint, and installs it along with a wood stove from the local feed store.

Butch's artwork, which is shown internationally in galleries, is found throughout the house. There are ancestral portraits he found and painted over with X-ray-like skeletons, bird and fish sculptures made of objects such as his grandmother's butter churn lid, and large "bowl sculptures" woven from bones, scrap metal and beaver-gnawed sticks.

Natalie Chanin, who shares the house part-time with Butch and their young daughter Maggie, also shares in the make-it-yourself aesthetic. She is the owner of Alabama Chanin, a clothing design company in Florence, Alabama, which she began as a cottage industry, sewing out of her home. The couple follows do-it-yourself precepts to the maximum, from handmade houses and furnishings to hand-sewn clothing.

With his ability to see the beauty in commonplace objects and transform them by taking them out of a mundane context, Butch has made a unique and finely crafted home with his own hands, doing it on his own terms, and in his own way.

On the table is a fish sculpture Butch Anthony made from scraps, including the lid of his grandmother's butter churn. On an old fireplace cover he painted a portrait of a woman.

OPPOSITE ABOVE: *The tin-roofed house is built of timber salvaged from an old cotton mill. On the patio are a couple of red metal gliders, which Butch says, "were once ubiquitous, but now are getting hard to find."*

OPPOSITE BELOW: *Liberty bib overalls, part of Butch's signature outfit, hang to dry on a clothesline strung up on the porte cochere. An assortment of old chairs used for sitting outside is stashed up under the roof.*

LEFT: *Hanging on a peg is a "mule chair," a traditional Alabama porch-sitting chair. Butch finds and repairs these, weaving new seats out of old neckties or cut up T-shirts. A bird sculpture he made sits on top of a stack of the old toolboxes he collects.*

RIGHT: *Bentwood chairs and table purchased from a picker are at home on a screened porch. Hanging as a chandelier is a Christmas tree Butch made out of scrap iron, "with weird things dangling down, such as sweetgum balls and rattlesnake rattles."*

In the living room sits a birdhouse made out of scrap wood by a friend. Butch tore apart some old kitchen cabinets to make the coffee table, while a carpenter's toolbox is used as an end table. A hand-planed 1850s wardrobe was found in a barn down the road.

OPPOSITE ABOVE: A mixture of clay, mortar and sand was filled in between the amber-colored heart pine timbers, producing a striped effect. The ladder leads to a small library loft.

OPPOSITE BELOW: Finding an old bedspring in the woods and liking its sculptural quality, Butch brought it home and hung it on a living room wall. He picks up handmade 1930s depression-era quilts "for cheap" and stacks them; at one time he had 75 in a pile.

Countertops in the kitchen were made from heart pine window frames that were joined and sanded down. Butch likes to cook "things like butterbeans and cornbread, using lots of stuff out of the garden."

Butch painted the sitting room floor in a geometric pattern inspired by the Escher-like doodles he did as a kid. He mixes 1950s couches and lamps with old-fashioned chairs.

LEFT: *The front stoop, ornamented with a salvaged piece of wrought iron, uses an old millstone as a step. The arched windows came out of a local church; one of them has a bullet hole in it.*

Butch's summer bedroom has a floor of painted cement and walls of stucco.
The bed's platform is made from painted car tags and old metal Alabama road
signs found at the dump.

A downstairs bedroom contains an old armoire and a cowhide rug from a yard sale. Butch gathers chewed-upon sticks from beaver dams, bleaches them and turns them into elegant sculptures. The teeth marks leave interesting little designs on the sticks.

OPPOSITE ABOVE: *Two "dirty, frayed wing chairs found for $5 at the Possum Trot" have been revitalized with white house paint, which has aged nicely into a crackled, leathery finish. The armoire is a 1930s school locker sponge-painted to look like wood.*

OPPOSITE BELOW: *To allow light into a bathroom, Butch added windows screened with beaver-gnawed sticks, providing decoration and a bit of privacy. The white porch column from a tear-down Victorian is used structurally.*

A schoolhouse map serves as a window shade in the guest bedroom. A long bench against the wall is made of found lumber, designed and built by a friend. The plain and simple metal bed was found in an old house nearby. Above it, a niche built into the wall houses an artwork by Butch of an ancestor portrait painted over with a skeleton.

Suave and Simple

FOR MOST OF ITS 250 YEARS, the small cottage of Michael Leva, a fashion and beauty executive, was "just a sad, poor farmer's house, until finally it was abandoned."

Today, the wide-plank chestnut floors and original doors are still there, but the house has been transformed into a much more glamorous dwelling—first by a colonial homes enthusiast, and more lately by Michael, who has given it a very chic styling in his own sophisticated way.

Situated on top of a hill in Roxbury, Connecticut, and surrounded by stone fences, huge old maples and luxuriant gardens, the house is a 1765 saltbox variation of the Cape Cod cottage. Shaped according to this local historical style, the clean, plain lines of the house exterior construct a frame from the past for the spare, restrained decor within.

From the beginning, Michael felt he had entered into a personal partnership with the house and every element in it. Not wanting to stray too far from the roots of the house, he mixed old things with new. "I read voraciously about society decorators and the history of furniture and like to think that I carry on in the tradition of American decorators like Billy Baldwin and Van Day Truex, who were geniuses at mixing periods together," Michael says. Since the house was so small, he carefully considered and finessed the scale of items, creating a graceful sense of proportion. In the process, he used made-to-fit cabinetry and fine-boned furnishings that were well suited to the home's petite dimensions. Following a maxim to control, edit and distill, he furnished the rooms with restraint, choosing pieces such as a diminutive neoclassical settee and a small-scale chandelier.

Along with classical pieces, Michael blended in contemporary elements, including a 1950s Knoll couch, a '60s chrome lamp, metal garden chairs and a picnic table.

For the palette, Michael watched the light and colors of the sky and earth around him and chose paint and fabric based on what he saw: pale blues, silver grays, apple greens and many slightly different shades of white. He mixed soft pastels with bold jolts of color, adding drama with a fiery orange chair, a bright blue lamp, or deep black basalt Wedgwood pottery set against stark white walls.

Although the house is spare, the garden is dense and abundant. It teems with a mix of deep border gardens, hedges made out of vines, native perennials and exotic, deadly nightshades.

All in all, the house illustrates the paradoxical way in which complexity is sometimes required in order to achieve a suave simplicity. It's also an example of the mystery of elegance, knowing what to add and what to leave out.

Library shelves were built "just big enough to validate the small Swedish Gustavian sofa," keeping the proportions balanced within the tiny room.

LEFT: *For the breezeway, Michael designed a zinc and iron table; it holds a still life of peaches, hydrangeas and a hurricane lamp. Beneath it, an old basket is filled with espadrilles; above it hangs a lobster trap from Maine.*

RIGHT: *A walkway behind the house is "like a little private garden in itself," with privet hedge and jasmine, bay and fuchsia. Many of the plants are kept in terra cotta pots so that Michael can move them about.*

Situated in the Litchfield County hills, Michael Leva's house is a 1765 saltbox. Along with stone walls and ancient maples, the property has large border gardens, a patio, and a secluded swimming pool.

The living room mixes textures both smooth and rough, including a 1950s Knoll couch covered in velvet and 1960s metal Klismos garden chairs. A teal lamp made from a 1920s French display jar provides a jolt of color.

RIGHT: Garden lilies are set in front of a curved "witch eye" mirror. Hand-forged iron strap hinges on the door were saved; Michael says "those shards of black were needed in the room."

OPPOSITE ABOVE: A favorite 1782 Directoire double chair has a place in the center hall. Says Michael, "It's the epitome of neoclassical design, with every symbol of that period carved on it, including urns, shields, stars and acanthus leaves"

OPPOSITE BELOW: There are no electric lights in the dining room; at night it's lit only by candles and an early-nineteenth-century French chandelier. On the gracefully simple mantel are Swedish tole flower arrangers.

OPPOSITE: *Michael whitewashed the beams to brighten the kitchen and added 1920s mercury glass factory lights. Open cabinets display his Venetian and American glass collection from the early 1800s to the 1920s, with pieces in soft shades of blue, lilac and gray.*

ABOVE: *Next to French doors, Michael placed a picnic table along with 1930s neoclassical iron chairs. Lustrous black basalt Wedgwood provides a contrasting color within the all-white kitchen.*

LEFT: *An eighteenth-century American handmade wood confectioner's stand with an acorn finial was carved with gently cupped upper tiers.*

In an upstairs bedroom, a seating area consists of an orange-upholstered Louis Philippe chair, a Colonial Revival settee and a black Regency chair, all atop a simple jute rug.

RIGHT: In a corner, a lamp made from a blue French seltzer bottle sits upon a Swedish bureau. On the floor is a sheepskin rug sourced from a centuries-old Scottish sheep farm.

OPPOSITE: An upholstered linen bed is tucked in under the eaves of a small guest room. A 1970s smoked-glass bedside table is just large enough to hold a '60s chrome lamp and a small mercury glass ice bucket filled with flowers.

The secluded swimming pool was painted in several shades of blue, green and gray to give a stippled effect. A border garden of hydrangea, nicotiana, verbena and cardoons comes right up to the edge of the pool.

RIGHT: *Lush border gardens are 25 feet deep and include hardy native plants such as black-eyed Susan and echinacea.*

OPPOSITE ABOVE: *Fig vines and climbing hydrangea trained to grow on a fence around the pool create a faux hedge for privacy.*

OPPOSITE BELOW: *A box hedge, dividing the patio from the lawn, has been clipped into a whimsical caterpillar shape.*

Catskills Cottage

A WINDING AND NEARLY VERTICAL ROAD runs through the wild beauty of the Catskill Mountains above the Manor Kill stream in upstate New York. Perched on a steep hillside behind a wobbly picket fence is the color-filled aerie and retreat of Katherine Bowling and Paul Mutimear, an artist couple from Manhattan.

The Greek Revival, with its front door painted violet, was built around 1825, a time when painters of the Hudson River School were moving to cottages in this area of untamed wilderness to paint landscapes of mountains, rivers and pristine waterfalls. Katherine came for similar reasons, in love with the sublime aspects of nature she found there and to paint en plein air the blossoming trees, tangled thickets and solitary roads plunging off into far distances.

The landscape of her childhood had been quite different. Born in Virginia, she grew up on the water on the eastern shore of Maryland, clamming, crabbing and sailing. Now, although her house is set in splendid isolation high on a mountain and not on a beach, it's as if the place, the color and the light she was born with have somehow been recaptured here. The house is painted sea foam green on the outside and contains many shades of ocean blue within. Paintings of sea-going vessels and items with nautical motifs seem perfectly at home.

For Katherine, who always dreamed of having a house of her own, there is a sense of childhood familiarity and memory in this place. And there is also a kind of romance to the house, with its poetics of enchanted space, of small cottages in folkloric tales set remotely in deep woods or high atop mountain turrets.

"Coming from a large family of five kids, there was always chaos around me; I was the loner in the group and craved solitude," Katherine says. "My very first drawings were done on the sly, drawn on walls in secret places, always of a house with two windows, a chimney emitting curly smoke and two trees and a walkway."

Nature surrounds and embraces the house on all sides. Katherine's garden includes the thousands of wildflowers that bloom on the side of the mountain in spring. Light flickers in through wisteria vines and lilacs, creating shadows on the floors. The French doors in the kitchen open to a deck with a view of a vast domain of sky, clouds and distant hills.

Throughout the house are mementoes of her past, especially of her grandmother's house from which she has brought garden gnomes, old-fashioned metal lawn chairs, etched glassware and sailor dolls.

Like most people with old houses in the Catskills, Katherine has found her furnishings not in stores, but at auctions, yard sales and flea markets. But with her own strong imagination, she has given each thing a charge; the inanimate objects seem to speak and exert a magical spell.

Alchemical vases line the walls; there is a copy of a letter from a prince on a wall; a monster in a painting guards a door; and a stuffed deer head has been adopted and given a name. It seems that the vision of her childhood and the house she once imagined owning has been fulfilled.

Around her 1825 Greek Revival, Katherine Bowling has planted a garden in a casual way, using cottage favorites such as hydrangeas, lilies, foxgloves and hollyhocks.

Though Katherine is not an advocate of deer head trophies, she felt sorry for this moth-eaten one from a yard sale and gave it a home. The Union Jack pays homage to Paul, who was born in England.

Katherine, who has a penchant for eclectic Moroccan objects, found the small Moorish-style table at a nearby auction house. One of her landscape paintings hangs above the pillow-laden sofa.

LEFT: *The integrated dining/kitchen area has a round Stickley table that Katherine inherited from her family. Against the wall, three old bureaus with their tops cut off are placed side by side to form counter space.*

ABOVE: *A bright pink lantern hangs from a ship's wheel lamp, while bookshelves hold all manner of books. "If I could live in a room filled only with books, I'd be quite happy," Katherine says.*

The cabinet holds etched glassware from Katherine's grandmother Minnie "that no one else in the family wanted." Walls are painted Buckland Blue, a popular house color in the nineteenth century.

RIGHT: *A painting of a hirsute "monster, caveman or Bigfoot" was rescued from a Montauk, NY, sale for ten cents and became "the symbolic soul and conscience of the house." Striped tea towels hung on a twig cover a storage cubbyhole.*

"The kitchen was grungy with 1970s foulness when I first saw the house," Katherine says. A big vintage sink bought for ten dollars replaced the old one, and fresh coats of white and blue paint brightened the space.

Matte-glaze vases in numerous shades of blue and white were all purchased for ten dollars or less at yard sales. A curvaceous black chair was found tossed out on the street in New York City.

RIGHT: Having grown up in the Tidewater region of Virginia, Katherine's love of the sea and sailing is evidenced by a collection of beach, ship and lake scenes, some of which are paint-by-numbers.

OPPOSITE: Nautically themed objects, such as the twin anchor sconces, seem to find her wherever she goes. A piece of crochet work is displayed on a chair back, just to show all the intricate work that has gone into it.

The amethyst color of a guest bedroom was taken from an old wisteria vine growing outside the window. After buying the bureau, Katherine painted it with buttermilk paint, then waxed and distressed it.

OPPOSITE A twig chair in a guest bedroom was purchased on the spot from the back of a delivery truck at a highway rest stop. Yard sale vases line up on a beam; most of them made in Ohio potteries such as Roseville, Hull and McCoy.

Writer's Retreat

"THE HOUSES INHABIT YOU, and not the other way around," says Eric Kater. "They gradually take you over." Kater's rambling cottage, where he lives along with his partner, Susan Welber, was begun in 1785 as a single room over a stone basement and then "sprouted in all directions".

Seeking a weekend retreat from New York City, writer Eric at first thought the house in the quiet hamlet of Oak Hill, New York, was not at all what he was looking for. It was too big, too close to the road and didn't have enough land. It also needed a lot more work than he wanted to put into it. But upon looking more closely and noticing its age and quaint details, as well as all of its quirks, he realized he would be hard-pressed to find another house quite as unique. "It seemed to have been well built, a place where things were done expediently, but always with an eye kept on costs," he says approvingly.

The house had a long and storied history. It had been built and added on to in three stages, and it had formerly been a tearoom, a telephone office, an apartment house and an antique store. Legend says that one Thomas Adams, a close relative of President John Adams, had owned it in 1798 and had manufactured nails there. And there was rumor of a ghost who liked to knock books off shelves during the night.

In furnishing the house, Eric says he found his way intuitively. "The house was all about wearing its age, and it told me what it wanted me to do," he says. He was particularly enamored of all the wood in the house—the rich Georgian fielded paneling in the oldest part, and the wide floorboards of ancient hemlock dating back to the days when the village had a tannery.

Eric found himself ripping out a 1960s bathroom and lining its walls with wood. He took away a ceiling above the living room and left the wooden beams in place; he allowed the rough horizontal wallboards in other rooms to remain. He also picked up utilitarian wooden workmen's tables that came out of local workshops and barns.

Coming from a family of sailors and sea captains and liking things built in an orderly, ship-like fashion, Eric preferred a no-nonsense approach to the decor. He built a balcony from which one could perch as in a ship's crow's nest. He worked to eliminate the unnecessary wall stencils added by a former owner. Eschewing all frou-frou, he developed "a manly look and feel to the place, a noirish feeling of women, bars, ships, and that kind of thing."

When painfully scraping paint off some surfaces, at some point he says he "just gave up because it wasn't ever going to come off, and at some point you just have to do what the house wants and give in." And that was all for the best, because now the house, clad in all its wood, has much pleasing texture as well as patina.

"The house has been my salvation and my downfall," Eric says. "It's taken up more time and effort than I ever expected myself to put up with. But it's also been very satisfying and fun. And in the process, I've found out things about myself that otherwise I would never have known."

An antique table holds "a World's Fair whiskey bottle and assorted boxes concealing booze and tobacco." The lamp has a shade with a floating wheat pattern and a base of "a very manly man with a scythe, cheerfully reaping."

OPPOSITE ABOVE: *In the center of the house, a lounge area is a place to relax in a red vinyl 1940s chair from a barbershop.*

OPPOSITE BELOW: *Eric Kater's 1785 cottage was built in the Dutch manner with bent framing. At one time Oak Hill was a prosperous village with mills, iron foundries and fashionable homes; eventually, it lapsed into a place where time seems to have stopped architecturally in the late 1800s.*

Eric, who says his decorating style is an intuitive "whatever-catches-my-eye style," picks up things he's drawn to at local auctions, yard sales and flea markets

OPPOSITE: *The kitchen is situated in a lean-to addition of the house. A wooden table came from a workshop in a barn; another table was custom made with a built-in bench, "meant to be very ship-like."*

LEFT: *Eric removed the glass from the Victorian-era china cabinet and now uses it as a catchall. The big copper pot is used for "cooking bouillabaisse, lamb stews and other dishes that are in no hurry to get done."*

Sometime around 1830, a one-room addition was built onto the house to provide a formal dining room; in later years it was used as the switchboard office for the local telephone company.

RIGHT: *Finding the blue paint impossible to remove, Eric gave up and, liking the patina, realized he had stopped at exactly the right time. The oddly built stairs are "in keeping with the unique qualities of the house."*

OPPOSITE: *Whatnot shelves are built into a former exterior window above a cocktail bar called the Mystery Bar, in honor of Eric's collection of noir novels.*

In a downstairs bedroom, there is "an oddball coupling of a late Victorian slipper chair and a kooky chair painted gold; both of them remarkably uncomfortable."

OPPOSITE ABOVE: Bright green walls and a blue floor illustrate Eric's theory that strong, saturated colors contrast well with dark wood furniture.

OPPOSITE BELOW: In the bathroom, Eric scraped off layers of wallpaper to reveal the wooden walls and updated with a soapstone sink that came from a high school lab.

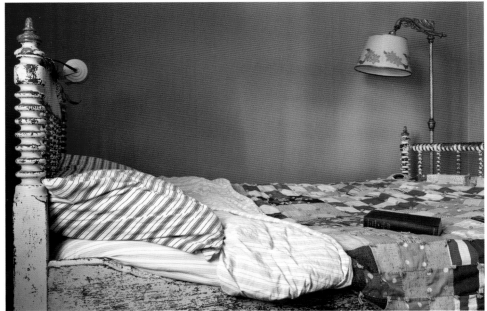

OPPOSITE: Eric got rid of the living room ceiling, keeping the beams. Perched above the room like a crow's nest, a small balcony is used as a sleeping quarter.

ABOVE: A wall in the oldest room was finished in late Georgian style with painted, fielded panels. The painting of a woman tenderly holding a goose was found at auction for $20, complete with frame.

LEFT: "The pumpkin color of the walls creates a kind of warmth," says Eric, who doesn't shy away from color in his house.

Hayward Cottage

SITED DIRECTLY ON THE CRAGGY COASTLINE OF RHODE ISLAND, Hayward Cottage has survived many storms. It is weathered, salt-encrusted and infused with the sight and sound of the sea.

"We don't think of the cottage as being anything special, but the view is truly spectacular," says Robin Lloyd, a filmmaker and a member of the extended family who now shares the house. It has belonged to the Lloyd family for nearly three generations, with many years of wet towels, bathing suits and tracked-in sand that's been swept back out of its many doors.

The house is a composite of several small buildings that were first put together in the 1940s by actress Beatrice Herford and her husband Sidney Hayward. In the early '60s Mary Lloyd, Robin's aunt and the daughter of William Bross Lloyd and Lola Maverick, both renowned peace and civil rights activists, purchased the cottage from Beatrice. By the 1970s Mary Lloyd had left the house to her three siblings, who decided they would all share the cottage along with their children and now grandchildren.

Unapologetically old-fashioned, the cottage is very plainspoken in its materials and rustic in its details. Robin says, "We haven't made the interior very elegant, as we expect the whole place might be washed away due to climate change before long." The house is in a tenuous position from any rise in sea level, and its architectural nature is fragile in the wake of heavy storms. Yet the cottage remains a steady constant in the lives of those who come here each summer.

The great appeal of the cottage is the informality that comes from the way it was built of humble materials, with nothing fancy or jarringly new added on and nothing extraneous or bothersome. At Hayward Cottage, simple charm is pronounced with the mismatched sofas, wicker furniture, old chairs, painted floors and chenille-covered beds that came with it.

The kitchen is small and unfussy, keeping vacation work to a minimum. As Robin says, "none of the family is that big on large-scale hospitality." Meals are casual and unplanned, with the family preferring to bicycle over to the fishermen's boats and the vegetable stand to see what's available for simple dinners of freshly caught fish.

Foraging has also been a longstanding tradition here. Robin relates that one of her aunts used to make rose hip jam from the wild rose bushes growing along the beach; another aunt used to wade out into the water and dive for mussels, bringing them back in a swimsuit.

Towels are hung from hooks along the wall, ready to take to the beach or the outdoor shower, where you can luxuriate under a stream of warm water while looking up at the sky. Thin vintage wool blankets, neatly folded on shelves, wait for a chilly night.

Welcoming and generous in spirit, the house is remembered for providing shelter to its extended family. It lets in the elemental sounds of crashing waves, sea gulls and migrating swans, as well as salt breezes and misty fogs. But the primary thing is always the water's proximity, and the hopes that it will withstand.

In the largest bedroom, a plain ladder-back chair, fold-down shelf, and small cabinet are all that's required, along with a straw hat and plaid wool blankets "that never seem to wear out."

The shore hugs the isolated and remote cottage, which is built into a landscape of rocky promontory, saltwater ponds, marsh and stone wall-bounded farms. Wild rose bushes form a tangled barrier, separating land from sea.

RIGHT: A large picture window in the open living/dining room shows the home's proximity to the sea. Above the fireplace is a painting by a local artist illustrating the curving road along the coast leading to Hayward Cottage.

The dining area has old-fashioned chairs, a simple wooden
table and a built-in bench under a big window. Floors
and doors are painted ocean blue; the walls and ceilings
have been left rough wood, without any insulation.

The cottage was built on the rocky coast of Rhode Island sometime in the 1940s by Sidney Hayward and his wife Beatrice Herford, who was a famous monologue artist in her day. The core of the house was originally a one-room shingled cottage to which several additions were made.

LEFT: *Almost every room in the cottage has a door with direct egress to the beach. "Keeping them all open throughout the day allows one to hear the ocean waves and early morning birds," Robin says.*

A generously sized yellow dresser in the dining area is easy storage for everyday items as well as a vehicle for display. It holds brightly colored sets of family pottery, including a tea service made by a potter in Vermont.

RIGHT: The shingled wall was once the exterior of the original house. Fishing poles are used infrequently. Robin says, "It's quicker to bicycle down to the point and buy some fresh fish just coming in off the fishing boats."

OPPOSITE: The small kitchen used to be even smaller, consisting of just a service area with a wooden counter. It's been modernized simply with new cabinets, a sink and blue countertops. Seen through a window is an outdoor shower, one of summer's great pleasures.

In the bunkroom, a blue dresser holds sewing and reading materials to occupy oneself with.

LEFT: *A cozy bedroom was the one chosen by Aunt Mary Lloyd; she also had a small cabin behind the house that she used as her writing studio.*

OPPOSITE: *In the morning, the bedroom door is opened, a chair is taken out onto the deck and a cup of coffee can be enjoyed. An heirloom piece of Victorian furniture is tucked against a wall and has been there since the Hayward days.*

Whaler's Cottage

"WHEN I FOUND MY ANCIENT WHALER'S COTTAGE so many years ago, Sag Harbor was a little whaling town, forgotten by time," says Peter Acocella, who inhabits the historic Hulbert/Coles house along with Aaron Brown.

Since the early 1700s, Sag Harbor, NY, has been a fishing village with an atmosphere steeped in history and a rich variety of architectural styles that gives evidence of its age. There are colonial-era "half-houses," whaling ship captains' Greek Revivals, sea merchants' red brick Georgian mansions and even an Egyptian Revival church with a "blubber spade motif" (named for the once all-important tool.)

With adventuresome whalers seeking pods of whales all the way to the Far East and the Arctic Ocean, the town revolved around a prosperous sea trade long before it became a stylish summer resort.

This tiny saltbox, built on the waterfront in 1740, was once a ship's store for the sloop Mehitable, whose owner Captain John Hulbert did business with the West Indies. Around two hundred years ago, the house was moved from the wharf to its present location in the center of town.

It is now the home of Peter and Aaron, who fully appreciate the charm of owning an historic small house rather than one of the new McMansions going up nearby. Its jewel box—like size brings with it a limited amount of possibilities but also the opportunity to create a small ordered world of beauty within. In addition, it brings the tangible experience of living in the past.

"Mozart was writing his music in Vienna and this house was here. Imagine!" says Peter. He and Aaron have furnished the house with items selected for their links to the past, things rooted in a time that embraced formal beauty and custom.

In a cosmopolitan port, where exotic items were brought back by ship from foreign lands, the cottage follows suit with a Chinese export chair carved with sea serpents and a figure of a mandarin scholar from Shanghai. There is a mannequin doll from France that was once used to model hoopskirts made of whalebone, and goblets from a Moroccan bazaar.

Upon moving to their house, Peter and Aaron have experienced what it was like to live in the past, to sit in rooms lit only by candle and firelight, to store their wine in a small cellar lined with deerskin, and to garden using plantings that were popular in the 1700s.

They have known times in Sag Harbor when things were more laid back and "New Yorkers used to keep Woodie wagons out here at the train station and sand-filled jalopies for getting around town in washpants and an old sweater. And no one cared that a moth or two had taken a nibble out of that sweater."

Even though the town is not quite as casual or old school today, there is still a strong semblance to former times and a respect for history. As Peter says, he is "grateful to those custodians of the past, keepers of a time when life was simpler and just a bit kinder; a time when we appreciated the difference between patina and tarnish."

In the galley kitchen an antique standing desk is used as a storage container. The doll was a mannequin used by a French textile manufacturer; it was "dressed and taken out to the provinces to advertise the latest fashions."

OPPOSITE: *An unpruned privet hedge is "sculpture in winter and an umbrella in summer" for the brick-floored patio garden. Early 1900s cast-iron furniture "will still be there after a nuclear holocaust and is just about impossible to move."*

ABOVE: *The historic Hulbert/Coles house was built around 1740 on the Sag Harbor wharf. It was used as a ship's store for the sloop Mehitable before being moved to its present location in the center of the town.*

LEFT: *Aaron is an avid gardener, caring for the Franklinia, holly, magnolia, box and ivy in the patio area, where he encourages moss to grow on the old, irregularly shaped bricks. Peter says, "It is magical here. When the light is going down over the garden, it's just a place of great calm and natural beauty."*

OPPOSITE ABOVE: *A baking oven with two chambers is hidden behind the small door beside the fireplace. The wing chair is covered with "Four Continents" toile, a pattern adapted from the original from 1792.*

OPPOSITE BELOW: *A pair of portraits of a sea captain and his wife reside in the sitting room. A zinc rain barrel holding antique canes sits over a hatch door leading "to a deerskin-lined larder below, which is a great place to store wine."*

In the sitting room, heavy velvet curtains filter the harsh light of the present day. Reminders of Sag Harbor's maritime trade with the Far East include a Chinese chair made for the export trade, carved with undulating sea serpents. A portrait of a Native American chief also recalls the past.

An Irish cupboard holds a collection of pewter, Waterford and goblets from a Moroccan bazaar. The couple enjoy cooking in the small galley kitchen, although Peter says he "sometimes has a fit due to the lack of counter space."

RIGHT: Originally a saltbox, the house has an addition dating from the 1970s with skylights and two sets of French doors, all of which provide more light and communication between indoors and outdoors.

The loft, now a guest bedroom, was once the place where equipment for ship owner Captain Hulbert was stored. A bedside table was the first item Peter and Aaron bought for the house.

RIGHT: A steep, compact ladder stair to the loft above looks like it might have been built by a ship's carpenter and has a patina of many years of paint, as well as a rope hoist. Its scuffs indicate a long and admirable life of use.

OPPOSITE: The chimney was intentionally built to lean so that any water running down during storms would not fall directly onto the fire in the fireplace below. An Amish quilt on the bed was a gift from a frequent houseguest.

More Is More

THE HOUSE ON HEART'S CONTENT ROAD, set on many acres of meadows and woods in Catskill, New York, looks from afar like an ordinary kind of place. A couple of hundred years ago, it was a one-room affair where farmers eked out a living from the stony ground.

Presently, it is home to artists Portia Munson and Jared Handelsman and their two children, Zur and Freeda, and the place is anything but plain, simple or ordinary. The couple has created a home where "more is more," and where understatement and restraint have been jettisoned in favor of extreme decoration. Their cottage has fully evolved into a kind of "wunderkammer," a house of wonders, filled with objects d'art and ephemera and overflowing with joyful color and texture.

Having been in Portia's family since the 1930s, the house was home to her great-grandparents and then served as a hunting lodge for her father, uncle and their friends. She inherited it as an empty shell with "only a hand-operated water pump and a few beds, and no heat or insulation."

Though they "were completely broke at the time," Portia and Jared were not deterred and proceeded to make a home, using their imaginations and whatever came to hand.

Portia, inspired by a trip she had taken right after art school to Frida Kahlo's colorful house in Mexico, realized that she, too, wanted a house "that could be like an artwork in itself, a place where Jared and I could both work and develop our art."

Life, art and interior decoration quickly began to merge, with the entire environment of indoors and outdoors treated as artistic experimentation stations with an overall encompassing design of lavish embellishment and invention.

Wallpaper on a tight budget was no problem when a walk in the woods yielded scrolls of fallen white birch bark, which Portia then "glued to bathroom walls to cover ugly tiles."

Jared planted hundreds of blueberry bushes in a huge double spiral shape, creating an environmental sculpture as well as providing berries to barter for goat cheese. Trees were tapped for maple syrup, wood was chopped and used to cook and heat the house, and flowers were grown and used in Portia's artwork of vibrant mandalas composed of multicolored blossoms.

Many old family heirlooms were incorporated; other furnishings were luckily found discarded by the side of the road. All were carefully curated and arranged with a sense of placement that was the result of much contemplation and concentration. As Portia says, "I really care about what I am looking at."

The love of opulence carried out as well into their gardens, where they made tree houses, mazes, vine-covered pergolas to dine in and small huts for bathing and showering.

While Portia and Jared know they might be accused of coming down with a bad case of "horror vacui," their dislike of unadorned, empty space has led to the creation of a home that is a true artistic statement and one that is always visually satisfying.

The wraparound sun porch has a sink with an operable hand pump used for "washing dirty vegetables coming in from the garden and for flower arranging."

ABOVE: *The cedar clapboard house in Catskill, New York, began as a one-room subsistence farmer's home about 300 years ago. In 1931, Portia Munson's great-grandparents moved here from Brooklyn to pursue a rural life, raising pigs and turkeys and growing vegetables in their garden.*

BELOW: *Jared has planted hundreds of blueberry bushes in a huge double spiral shape. Posts hold up the netting that keeps birds away from the berries until harvest. Besides providing bushels of berries for bartering, the spiral is a beautiful environmental artwork.*

*Laundry hangs out to dry on a clothesline with the North
Mountain of the Catskills appearing in the background
of their 83-acre garden and woodland.*

LEFT: *Used in winter for "hunkering down and reading," this room in the oldest, center part of the house has a wood-burning stove. The chimney has been tiled with blue and white, while the doors and cupboard have been given a faux bois treatment by Portia.*

The living room's rocking chair and Victrola both belonged to Portia's great-grandparents. On the mantel of the brick fireplace sits a porcelain clock sculpted with delicate flowers, made by the ceramics artist Ann Agee.

An Indonesian daybed is almost totally obscured by a blue sheepskin and a mass of colorful pillows made by Portia. Jared says the room "is a cul-de-sac of items, representing a good cross section of generations of the family."

RIGHT: Portia covered the walls and ceiling of a downstairs bath with peeling curls of white birch bark found on their land. Artwork by the couple is hung on the walls.

OPPOSITE: In the living room, Portia created her own wallpaper by stenciling the walls with flowers. When that did not seem quite decorative enough, she photocopied and enlarged pictures of pansies from old greeting cards and applied them to the walls.

OPPOSITE: *In the mornings, Jared gets the fire going in the Red Cross Prize woodstove with wood that he chops and stores in a vast spiral-shaped pile outside. The colors of potholders made by Portia echo the braided rug made by her grandmother.*

ABOVE: *Eggs from their Bantam hens sit on a cast-iron sink the couple found at a salvage house. Barbershop ads from Nigeria hang on the wall along with watermelons painted by Portia.*

LEFT: *The pantry, with its floor and cupboard stenciled with daisies by Portia, stores food and other supplies, including wine kept inside the old bureaus. Kerosene lamps were used in the house; until the 1980s the house had no electricity.*

An upstairs bedroom has two double beds pushed together. The barrel chairs, which Jared says "have gone through hell," have had a long life of use and belonged to Portia's great-grandparents.

RIGHT: *A salvaged stained glass window slides open to look down onto the sun porch. Portia found the standing lamp at a yard sale and gave it a white leather Indonesian shade.*

OPPOSITE: *In the upstairs bath, a cast-off sink found by the side of a road has been placed on a favorite small table. Fern-patterned linoleum was there from Portia's grandparents' time.*

Crossroads Cottage

WEST FULTON, NEW YORK, a village formerly known as Sapbush Hollow, is a place rich in natural beauty, local color and history. Once a busy crossroads, the town used to have a hotel, a church hall with a theater, a general store with an ice cream window and an old-fashioned tourist attraction of waterfalls. Time passed and many buildings were abandoned as farmers, craftspeople and shop owners picked up and moved to cities or went out West.

Lately, a handful of people coming from New York City and beyond have been discovering the buildings from the mid-1800s that were left behind, some now in various stages of repair and one quite perfect in its completed renovation.

This was the case with Kat Schaufelberger and Zak Orth, who were not seriously looking to buy a house until they noticed a small white cottage for sale by the side of the road and became smitten with its sweet charm. They were the first to look at the property, and after only five hours decided they would take it. "We didn't want it to get away," says Zak, "we knew if we let it go, we'd think about it and regret it for the rest of our lives."

A former blacksmith shop, the house in previous lives had been a gas station and then a radio repair shop, with the shop owners and their five children living upstairs in quarters above the garage. After that, it became the residence of an art gallery owner, who passed it on to two style consultants from New York City, thus giving the space a provenance of artistic improvers.

The house had been furnished throughout with things that had been locally sourced from the surrounding area, including a church lectern, a notched-edge table once used for weaving, vintage appliances and an old-fashioned porcelain sink. "We bought it furnished and completely 'as is' from the owners of the design company Aesthetic Movement." says Zak, "In fact, we insisted that the inclusion of all the furnishings would be one of the conditions of the sale."

The house came with a collection of chairs "painfully selected by the former owners over a period of twelve years," including Cuban Deco ones, firehouse Windsors, Hitchcocks, and antique milking stools from nearby dairy farms. Things that had come out of local attics and cellars were joined with Kat and Zak's family pieces, all adding to the retrospective mood of the interior. Kat's grandmother's prized Rosenthal china fills the glass-doored cabinets in one room, while her baby grand piano, given to her by her grandfather on her thirteenth birthday, fits easily into the large room that once housed cars.

Today, the crossroads is quiet at night and the house has a peaceful vibration that the couple is very attuned to. Says Zak, "It really feels like paradise, with everything just a bit off-plumb and kind of faded and leaning. Time just stopped here in the perfect place."

Kitchen shelving holds everything from candlesticks to Kat's grandmother's martini shaker; antique milking stools are stored beneath it. Zak is so fond of the old-fashioned orange juicer that he is "threatening to start a collection of them."

OPPOSITE ABOVE: *Built in the mid-1800s, the house in West Fulton, NY, has had various incarnations as a blacksmith shop, a service station and a radio repair shop. The old storefront windows are still intact, screened by a planter.*

OPPOSITE BELOW: *Behind the house a deck was built on top of river stones; hydrangeas and ferns were added, providing a tranquil setting. At night, Zak and Kat say they "can hear cows, coyotes and the creek."*

The large, open living/dining area of the house was once a garage where vehicles were repaired. Kat and Zak purchased the home complete with all the furnishings from the previous owners; added to the existing pieces were a sofa and a baby grand piano.

The kitchen, which used to be a shop's office, was renovated with vintage appliances, custom shelving and a freestanding butcher's block. A 1950s GE refrigerator has been raised up on a cupboard, providing extra storage space beneath.

Kat and Zak like to entertain, with Zak often making his "Upstate Soup" for friends and weekend guests who gather in the kitchen. The Wincroft brand stove has been converted to propane.

LEFT: *Sometime in the 1990s, a cast iron sink "weighing about 800 pounds" was installed in the kitchen. A vintage lighting fixture is reflected in one of the many "shaving mirrors" found throughout the house.*

The former upstairs kitchen is now used as a sunny drawing room. A still life painting of roses in a vase, displayed on an artist's easel, was once in Kat's grandmother's house.

RIGHT: The cupboards and sink of the original kitchen have been retained for their vintage quality and come in handy for extra storage and washing up. An embroidered pillow on the striped wing chair shows a tugboat with an octopus aboard.

OPPOSITE: A pair of firehouse Windsor chairs was a gift from a friend. Made in the early 1800s, they've been strengthened with metal tighteners, a utilitarian way of repairing old chairs.

OPPOSITE: *The portrait of an unknown man with a commanding presence "has been named Edward and is now the guardian of the house."*

In a bedroom, the built-in cabinets with glass handles are original fixtures; they hold Kat's collection of Rosenthal china from her grandmother. A patchwork quilt that was handmade long ago in Schoharie County covers the spool bed.

Setting the Scene

MISE-EN-SCENE, the French term for the placing of things on stage, is a good description of the way Bob Topol and Tony Trotta have gone about designing their country place in the historic town of Morris, Connecticut. Both are talented scenic art directors, responsible for creating the look and style of many Hollywood films. At work, Bob and Tony deal with the arrangement of all the things that appear within the frame of a movie scene: its décor, props and lighting, all of which are crucial to setting the tone of a film.

The couple is known for their ability to create a convincing sense of time and place using their historical knowledge along with a lot of improvisation. "The things we learn at work, we then take home with us," Bob says.

After looking at many houses, the one they finally settled on was "just a small, 1962 fake log house." But because the property was located close to a lake and because they were both admirers of the Adirondack style, they thought the place had potential and began to work their magic on it.

Their first idea was to "make it a sort of rustic lake house." They created a dining room as an "ode to the Great Camps," by keeping the woody, dark log walls and adding some Craftsman-like touches.

Taking another artistic leap, they continued in the Arts & Crafts vein and added a wing, this one in the Shingle style, circa 1910. Built as a perfect square, the new addition has French doors on every side, transoms, a big stone chimney and a balcony with a portico beneath it.

Elements of an English country house crept in, creating in the process an imagined ancestral history for the house. Coats of arms, etchings, collections of teapots and decorative china plates were introduced, along with chintz-covered chairs and a profusion of cushions.

Constantly traveling to different film locations, Tony and Bob took notes on all they saw, accumulating things wherever they went. They brought back paintings and candlesticks from Italy; they got ideas from visiting old inns in New England. After a trip to the Caribbean, loving the tropical ambience of a cottage they had stayed in, they added on an airy kitchen with high ceilings, lemon yellow walls, white-painted beams and cobalt blue tiles

They painted glass panes with French lacquer to imitate stained glass, a technique they developed for a church scene in the film *Clockers*. A beam that was used on the set of a slave cabin in the movie *Beloved* was installed as a mantel. The props from film sets and the things that came from their families and friends, along with treasures brought back from trips eventually made a comfortable cottage with all the iconic aspects of a country home.

Today, it's a living space that is always a theater for innovation and improvisation, one that keeps changing as new inspirations arrive. As Bob says, "a decorator never stops decorating, and when you're designing something, you never stop looking."

Over the blue-tiled fireplace, Bob Topol and Tony Trotta placed a sign bearing a coat of arms that came from an Irish pub in Hudson, New York, and had been used as a movie prop. The travelers palm trees are taken inside during the winter.

LEFT: *Bob and Tony added an Arts & Crafts Shingle-style wing to their country place in Morris, Connecticut. The balcony, which has a door to their bedroom, is where they breakfast; the portico is "another place to be outdoors and to have cocktails in the evening."*

ABOVE: *The pool house design was inspired by the garden entrance of the Rodin Museum in Philadelphia. It consists of two pavilions joined together by an open-air porch.*

The living room addition, built as a perfect square, has French doors and transoms on all four sides. An Egyptian funerary mask made in the first century of cartonnage presides on the mantel; above it a painting titled Columbia came from the lobby of an old theatre in upstate New York.

The brocade covered wing chair in the library was purchased while on location in Charleston "because it had such a royal quality about it."

Bob and Tony had a fireplace built for the library using a beam from the set of a slave cabin. A bust of Shakespeare came from Bob's father; marble candlesticks were once used in a church in Italy.

The kitchen addition, with its wall of windows, has a 14-foot ceiling; it was inspired by a cottage the couple rented in the Caribbean. A collection of teapots is displayed on recycled beams cut from local trees.

RIGHT: A potted geranium grows in a sunny window on a counter above storage cupboards. Tiffany plates hung on the wall "mark the centennial of the journey of Christopher Columbus."

The kitchen island was constructed with a granite top; on one end it is made from an old cashier's desk with many drawers. The "stained glass" panes are actually painted French lacquer; they were created for the movie set of a church scene.

In the hall that connects the old and new parts of
the house, green-and-white-checked curtains enclose
the entrance to the dining room. A butler's pantry is
hidden in one of the closets.

RIGHT: The entry hall has a bench from a friend's estate
covered in a fabric designed by Jack Lenor Larsen. The
patterned rug came from Bob's parents' house and "just
happened to fit the space perfectly."

OPPOSITE: Keeping the log walls of the original part of
the house, the dining room was designed by Bob and
Tony to be "their ode to the great Adirondack camps."
The painting was brought back as the prize of a trip to
Italy.

Glazed walls in the upstairs bedroom are intended to create a Venetian plaster look. The seating area resembles an English country house, with chintz-covered chairs, coats of arms on the walls and an ottoman used for serving tea.

OPPOSITE ABOVE: Over the "very proper English rice bed" with its four posts is an English landscape painting. For a scene in a psychiatrist's office, Tony made a painting in the style of abstract expressionist Franz Kline.

OPPOSITE BELOW: Paul Newman falls asleep in this chair at the end of the movie Nobody's Fool. Tony and Bob have combined its chintz fabric with a cushion in a vivid French awning stripe.

Acknowledgments

Many thanks to the owners of the houses in this book, who allowed us to photograph their homes and shared their stories with us.

For their help in producing this book, we are especially grateful to Margaret Tirpaeck, Glenn Petry and the Pridwin Hotel, Tom Luciano and Mary Lou and Nick Nahas.

Sincere thanks to Cindy and Jim Barber for always finding flowers in a pinch, to Rosi and Michael Smith for Alabama lodgings, and to Jack Bashkow and Lorraine Shemesh for holding down the fort while we were on location.

Thanks also to Glenn Gissler, Craig Strulovitz, Stephen Shadley, Joe Haske, Marjorie Van Dyke, Marilynn Karp, Jennie Chastain and Stephen Bernstein for their enthusiasm and delicious repasts.

We also acknowledge Madge Baird and Melissa Dymock for their assistance in the successful completion of this project.

Our deepest thanks to Edith Gross for her invaluable support and good cheer.

For Edith, with love